THE INDUCTION POCKETBOOK

2nd Edition

C000066420

By Ruth Sangale & Philippa Webster

Drawings by Phil Hailstone

"Clear, concise, thought provoking and captures the essence and essential ingredients of a sound induction process. Although a small book, it is full of useful tips, which if followed will ensure there are minimal problems during the process."

Elaine McFarlane, Head of HR, The CBI

"A delightfully succinct handbook packed with easily-digestible and jargon-free advice and practical checklists, while reflecting the diverse nature of work and workforces, latest technology and long-term approach to employee engagement."

Elizabeth J Smith, HR Manager, Cafédirect plc

Published by:
Management Pocketbooks Ltd
Laurel House, Station Approach, Alresford, Hants SO24 9JH, U.K.
Tel: +44 (0)1962 735573   Fax: +44 (0)1962 733637
E-mail: sales@pocketbook.co.uk
Website: www.pocketbook.co.uk

First edition: 2000 © Ruth Sangale
ISBN 1 870471 81 4

This edition 2007 © Ruth Sangale & Philippa Webster
ISBN 978 1 903776 82 7

British Library Cataloguing-in-Publication Data – A catalogue record for this book
is available from the British Library.

Design, typesetting and graphics by **efex ltd**   Printed in U.K.

CONTENTS

INTRODUCTION 5
First impressions, stresses of a
new job, new beginnings, your
game plan, technology

**WHY HAVE AN
INDUCTION PROGRAMME?** 11
Maintaining motivation, theory of
motivation, objectives of induction,
benefits of good induction

WHO TO INVOLVE 23
Who is involved in the delivery of
induction and which staff should
receive induction training

**WHAT TO INCLUDE IN AN
INDUCTION PROGRAMME** 41
The four Ps – Place, Policy, Position
and People

HOW TO IMPLEMENT INDUCTION 55
Structure, length, culture, integrating
your culture, method of delivery
(written material, coaching, formal
training, group work, visiting
departments, buddying,
presentations, pilot)

**WHEN & WHERE INDUCTION
SHOULD TAKE PLACE** 83
Before starting, first day, next
few weeks, long-term needs,
what to bear in mind
regarding location

EVALUATING YOUR INDUCTION 93
Why, how (questionnaires,
checklists, line manager reports,
exit interviews) what to do with
evaluation results,
common feedback

Continued

CONTENTS

INDUCTION CHECKLISTS   105
Use these checklists when designing and implementing your induction programme. There's a checklist for each stage

CASE STUDY   115
How LBC successfully introduced a modular induction programme

SUMMARY   121
The main points of the book, together with useful mnemonics, summarised under seven headings

"There is new strength, repose of mind and inspiration in fresh apparel"

Ella Wheeler Wilcox

1NTRODUCTION

FIRST IMPRESSIONS

Catherine Brown arrived at the London head office of a global media company. She had secured the role of Accounts Director, based in Beijing, China, and had come to London, full of enthusiasm, for her induction. This was her experience:

- Arrived, jet-lagged, on Monday as instructed; receptionist had not been briefed
- Waited 30 minutes until the CEO's PA came to collect her
- After 10 minutes the CEO was called away, leaving Catherine with a cup of coffee, some company literature and accounts to mull over
- One hour later the CEO returned, apologised, and showed her around
- Went into a meeting where she met the other directors – the meeting was to discuss current client accounts and the loss of a major US client
- After a long lunch with the CEO, Catherine was given more company papers to read on the aeroplane
- At 19.00 she was on the flight back to China

Her impression: great to meet people, it's an exciting business but I'm not sure who my key contacts are for the client business and three months feels too long before my next meeting with the CEO. If you have had a similar experience, how did **you** feel?

INTRODUCTION

STRESSES OF A NEW JOB

Think back to the first day of your current job and the kinds of questions you asked yourself? Some of them may have been:

A good induction will help relieve some of the stress by answering these questions.

NEW BEGINNINGS

In the fast world of work, with new and speedier ways of communicating, expansion of global working and an increasing mix of cultures working together, facing a new job makes anyone feel anxious – some more than others. How you welcome, inform and integrate new staff will have an effect on the rest of their working time in your company. Therefore, the better the introduction, the easier it is for newcomers to settle in and identify the appropriate behaviour for success.

A good induction should **WIN** over your newcomers by:

W elcoming them to their new job, company and colleagues

I ntegrating them into the culture of the company

N avigating them around the company both physically and strategically

This book will guide you through the process by exploring the **why, who, what, how, when** and **where** of induction and by providing you with practical tips and examples of good practice.

INTRODUCTION

YOUR **GAME** PLAN

Whenever you are going to introduce a new procedure or process to an organisation, there are four things to think about at the planning stage:

G oal — What is the objective for this new process? Is it to inform, sell or persuade? What is the desired outcome?

A udience — Who are your audience? What are their needs, previous experience, are they newcomers, etc? Where are they: head office, a regional office or somewhere else on the globe?

M edia — What is the most appropriate method of communicating this process – talks, staff packs (on the intranet, a company CD-ROM or paper copies), video-conferencing? You will need to consider the location of the newcomer as this may require a different medium.

E xpression — Once a decision has been made about the medium, consider the best way of expressing the message – formal/informal, use of graphics, visual aids, use of quizzes, treasure hunts, team competitions, or a mix of all these?

INTRODUCTION

TECHNOLOGY

The use of technology is increasingly important in the successful implementation of induction programmes. With the expansion of the global workforce and workplace, newcomers may find themselves:

- Working with colleagues at a distance, be it at home or abroad
- Working in either a traditional face-to-face team or a virtual or remote team
- Being managed from a distance, only meeting their manager annually

When considering what to include in your induction programme (and how, when and where to implement it) the use of technology is key. It may include:

- Putting information about the company onto a company CD-ROM
- Placing more company information on the intranet
- More video-conferencing
- Greater use of email and telephone
- Interactive 'remote learning' on the newcomer's laptop or desktop

There are now IT packages and new telephone systems that allow high quality remote learning and, in the case of the latter, a reduction in telephone costs.

WHY HAVE AN
INDUCTION PROGRAMME?

MAIN GOAL: MAINTAIN MOTIVATION

Even though newcomers will be anxious, they will also be feeling enthusiastic and motivated to do a good job. The main goal of induction is to maintain this enthusiasm and motivation for as long as possible. This will result in a more effective performance.

You maintain motivation by providing your newcomer with:

- The right type of support and guidance
- At the right time
- In the right way
- In the right place

Throughout the book the term newcomer is used to include people who are new to a role – they may be a new starter in the company or may have been promoted or transferred from another office.

MASLOW'S THEORY

A newcomer's journey from being nervous and insecure to becoming a confident member of staff who can contribute to the goals of the company, can be compared to the steps in Maslow's Theory of Motivation.

Everyone has needs and Maslow believed that these needs could be arranged in a hierarchy starting off with basic physiological needs and ending with more intellectually demanding needs.

Until a need is satisfied, a person cannot (or is not motivated to) move on to the next level. It is the same with induction: before newcomers can begin to understand the more complicated aspects of their jobs and company, and before they can be fully effective, they need to be comfortable with some basic knowledge.

WHY HAVE AN INDUCTION PROGRAMME?

MASLOW'S HIERARCHY OF NEEDS

To understand the link with induction let's look at the needs:

- **Physiological** - basic biological needs, essential for survival, such as food, shelter and sleep

- **Safety** - includes protection from physical and psychological threats

- **Social** - the need for love, acceptance, friendship and social interaction

- **Ego** - includes a need for self-respect, confidence, recognition, power and competence

- **Self-actualisation** - self-fulfilment, achievement, realisation of potential

THE LINK BETWEEN NEEDS & INDUCTION

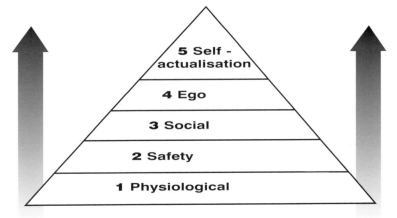

5 Self - actualisation

4 Ego

3 Social

2 Safety

1 Physiological

WHY HAVE AN INDUCTION PROGRAMME?

THE LINK BETWEEN NEEDS & INDUCTION

1 **Physiological** During the first few days newcomers require very simple, basic information in order to feel secure such as: knowing where they will be working, knowing who to contact regarding specific knowledge areas of the company, finding out where things are and learning people's names.

2 **Safety** Over the next few weeks they establish a routine and are given assignments with clear guidance. They now need to become familiar with the broader picture, eg the structure and aims of the company, the different departments, etc.

3 **Social** They then start forming relationships with people, by email if they are working from a distance, or having coffee or lunch with others. They begin to get used to the procedures and, therefore, to fit in.

4 **Ego** As they understand their roles better and attend development programmes, they start to gain self-respect and become more effective.

5 **Self-actualisation** After 6-12 months, with the right environment, newcomers should be fulfilling their potential within their roles.

(16)

OBJECTIVES OF INDUCTION: *COMPANY*

Different organisations have different induction objectives. Before introducing an induction programme you must first be clear about why you are doing it. Objectives mainly fall into three groups: *company-, job-* and *newcomer-*related.

Company-related objectives include giving an understanding of:

- **The company:** its culture, the culture of its employees, structure, products and clients
- **Policies and procedures:** health and safety, performance management, development, equal opportunities, diversity, pay, holidays, discipline and grievance, harassment and bullying etc
- **Work objectives:** departmental and company goals

OBJECTIVES OF INDUCTION: *JOB*

Induction enables newcomers to understand their roles better by providing an opportunity to:

- Get to know their manager

- Get to know the team they will be working with

- Meet colleagues with whom they may be working, although this needs to be flexible: eg with virtual teams who rarely or never meet and, for the most part, communicate via technology

- Receive development to enable them to carry out their roles

- Understand their job descriptions and how they fit in within the company

OBJECTIVES OF INDUCTION: *NEWCOMER*

- To provide a sincere welcome
- To put the newcomer at ease
- To give a good impression of the company
- To give an introduction to the culture of the company
- To integrate the newcomer effectively
- To give the newcomer skills and knowledge to do the job well

Your objectives for an induction programme may cover some or all of the aforementioned. Whatever your objective, a good induction programme will not only benefit the newcomer but will also benefit the company in many ways.

BENEFITS OF INDUCTION

TO THE COMPANY

Financial

Many people leave a job because they are disillusioned, let down or misinformed.
A good induction will illustrate to newcomers that the organisation is committed to
them and will do everything it can to retain them for as long as possible. This results in
reduction of staff turnover and recruitment costs.

Productivity

If newcomers are inducted well they will be able to respond quickly and effectively to
the demands of their new roles.

Effect on existing staff

Induction can have two effects on existing staff:

- they become more aware of the company's objectives by contributing or
  attending, and

- those contributing can improve their skills such as coaching and presentation

BENEFITS OF INDUCTION

TO THE NEWCOMER

Motivational
An induction programme should indicate what potential there is for growth and development within the organisation and how to capitalise on it. This will enable newcomers to work towards fulfilling their potential and, therefore, maintain their motivation.

Development
A good induction programme should include training for newcomers, whether that means learning the IT systems or learning English as a second language. It will encourage them to get involved and support development opportunities in the future. It will also make them effective in their roles faster.

Integration
Knowing how things are done in terms of accepted behaviour helps newcomers to integrate into the culture of the company and, indeed, know how to behave with other cultures now that we are working in a multi-cultural work environment.

DEVELOPMENT ACTIVITY

Get a team of volunteers together who can help research, design, develop, implement and monitor your induction programme – ensure different staff levels and locations within the company are represented. That done, decide on what your key objectives are for having your induction programme. Consider:

- When were these objectives last discussed and agreed?

- What has changed since, eg have you been through a merger and/or acquisition?

- Is a 'one-size fits all' induction programme appropriate for the whole organisation or does it need to be tailored to different regions, cultures, countries?

- Are some newcomers and their teams working in a virtual environment?

WHO TO INVOLVE

WHO TO INVOLVE
IN DELIVERY

A common mistake with induction programmes is to leave it all to one person to organise. This puts a lot of pressure on that individual and may reduce the effectiveness of the programme. It is advisable to involve as many people as you can in the process, by splitting the responsibility and making it more interesting.

Important people to involve are:

- Senior managers
- Supervisors or line managers
- Personnel or the person responsible for those issues
- IT department or the person responsible for IT
- Colleagues doing a similar role
- Colleagues from other departments with whom the newcomer may work

WHO TO INVOLVE

IN DELIVERY

Senior managers

You should always involve the most senior manager in the induction process because:

- It demonstrates that person's commitment to the process, and therefore …
- Other staff who are contributing to the induction will take it more seriously
- Newcomers are impressed that even the most senior member of staff has time to welcome them

The senior manager can assist in a number of ways:

- Provide a budget for the induction programme
- Give a presentation, either in person or on a company CD-ROM, about the company's history and future goals
- Meet the newcomer. If a small company, this may be face-to-face on the first day; if a larger company, it may be face-to-face on the next visit to a regional or international office or via a video-link.

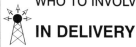

WHO TO INVOLVE
IN DELIVERY

Line managers

The line manager is probably the most important person in the induction process. This is the person the newcomer will be working for and the impression they make in the first few days will be a lasting one. It is essential, therefore, that the line manager allows enough time to spend with the new team member. Location is an important factor: if the newcomer is not based in the same office but works in a regional or international office, this needs careful planning. If a face-to-face visit is not possible in the first week, then technology may be the answer. For example, video-conferencing, a company CD-ROM, email and telephone contact, should all be considered.

In the first few weeks the line manager should:

- Make the newcomer feel welcome and at ease
- Introduce the person to the rest of the team
- Go through the job description and discuss team objectives and current projects
- Provide lots of opportunity for regular feedback
- Set some realistic objectives for the newcomer to achieve in the first 2-3 months

WHO TO INVOLVE
IN DELIVERY

Personnel department or person responsible

If your company does not have a personnel function then whoever is normally responsible for such matters should carry out this part:

- Check accuracy of the newcomer's details and issue a security pass if required
- Go through terms and conditions of employment
- Go over housekeeping rules and ensure they have a map of office/sites (this could be either a hard copy or on a company CD-ROM, for example)
- Introduce the newcomer to other personnel and admin staff
- Indicate how the newcomer can find relevant information and provide important telephone contact details

WHO TO INVOLVE
IN DELIVERY

IT department or person responsible

The IT department should:

- Ensure the newcomer's password is available on their first day
- Ensure their IT equipment is up and running on the first day
- Ensure they have adequate training on how to use the equipment – this could be face-to-face or via remote learning
- Ensure the company CD-ROM is up-to-date and available to the newcomer or is already loaded onto their desktop or laptop
- Ensure that any video-link or web-cam being used is all set up and ready to run
- Ensure that the technology used is cost-effective for telephone calls and remote learning

WHO TO INVOLVE
IN DELIVERY

Trainers

If your company is one where specialist skills are required in order for newcomers to be able to do their jobs, inform the trainer of the roles of the newcomers, their previous experience and relevant timing.

Development could include:
- Use of tailored IT systems
- Company writing style
- Presentation skills
- Consultancy skills
- Project management skills
- Customer care
- Filing systems
- Use of specialist equipment

The trainer may do this on a one-to-one basis, in a group development session or via remote learning.

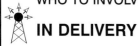

WHO TO INVOLVE
IN DELIVERY

Other staff

It may be useful to involve other staff and this can be done in several ways:

Job shadowing
Arrange for the newcomer to spend time with someone who is doing the same or similar job. This may help prevent mistakes or misunderstandings.

Buddying
Allocate to another member of staff the responsibility of offering support and guidance to the newcomer during his or her first few weeks.

Work placements
Let the newcomer spend time at different sites, for example on the shop floor or in the factory, so that the person can understand the work of other departments.

IN DELIVERY

DEVELOPING THOSE INVOLVED

Although those involved may be experts in their particular fields, don't assume that they will know how to impart their knowledge. Get everyone involved in the induction to come to a half-day workshop where you can go through:

- The aims and objectives of the induction programme
- The different parts of the induction and how they are linked
- Tips on presentation skills
- Guidelines on visual aids, or other equipment required
- Checklists of each person's role within the programme
- Coaching skills for line manager

It is important that everyone with a role goes through this to ensure complete understanding of the programme.

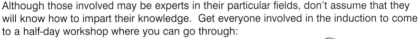

(31)

IN HAVING INDUCTION

Induction is not just for newcomers, but for anyone who is in a new situation at work or who has special needs. Induction, therefore, will include:

- Staff newly promoted
- Staff transferred
- Staff requiring re-orientation after major change
- People returning after a long break, eg: after illness or maternity leave
- Part timers/shift workers
- Those on temporary contracts
- Graduates/school leavers
- Work experience placements
- People on secondment

You must decide which parts of the induction will be relevant to them as they may not need all the information that a newcomer will receive.

IN HAVING INDUCTION

LOOKING AFTER DIFFERENT NEEDS

When designing your induction programme, allow it to be flexible to accommodate the different needs of staff. In particular:

- Women returning to work after a long break
- Graduates/school leavers
- Part-timers/shift workers
- Disabled people
- People on secondment and work experience
- Those transferred and promoted

WHO TO INVOLVE

IN HAVING INDUCTION

Women returning to work

Take into account the fact that:

- They may have lost confidence
- Their skills may be out of date
- They will need updating on company changes that have taken place while they were absent
- They may prefer one-to-one coaching rather than group training where they may feel unable to keep up with the rest of the group

WHO TO INVOLVE
IN HAVING INDUCTION

Graduates and school leavers

Some companies that hire large numbers of graduates will have a special graduate induction programme. However, this is not always necessary. What you need to think about is that many graduates have never worked before and, therefore, will need assistance with items that for others may seem unnecessary.

For example:

- How the photocopier and fax work
- Filing systems
- Dealing with customers and clients
- Change from academic style of working to a more pragmatic one
- How to meet deadlines within work hours

Remember, some may need confidence building and a buddy would probably help with this.

IN HAVING INDUCTION

Part-timers/shift workers

These people often get overlooked because they are not always available to attend the induction with other staff. However, it is important that they are treated in exactly the same way as a permanent newcomer would be by:

- Arranging training and presentations when they are able to attend
- Compensating them if they have to attend during their own time
- Allowing more time for them to get through the programme because they are not at work all of the time and, consequently, they may take longer to integrate

WHO TO INVOLVE
IN HAVING INDUCTION

Disabled people

It is now law that an employer carries out a risk assessment and may have to make reasonable adjustment(s) to accommodate disabled persons at work. The best way is to ask newcomers what it is they may need. This will depend on the disability but can include:

- Wheelchair access
- Special IT equipment such as larger screens, Braille keyboards, arm rests
- Signer

For more information on what is available, contact your local job centre.

IN HAVING INDUCTION

People on secondment and work experience

Even though these people are not permanent, it is still important that they are given the same introduction as permanent staff. This will enable them to be effective in what they are to achieve while they are with you.

Also it gives them a good impression of your company. Sometimes they may end up getting a job with you!

WHO TO INVOLVE
IN HAVING INDUCTION

People transferred and promoted

This is another group of people who tend to get forgotten. It is assumed that because they already work in the company they will not need induction. However, it is useful for these people to have:

- Information about their new role (a job description and explanation by the new manager and the setting of new objectives for the first 2-3 months in the new role)

- Introduction to the new team

- Integration into the team culture

- Development if new skills are required, for example, language or specialist IT skills.

NOTES

WHAT TO INCLUDE IN AN INDUCTION PROGRAMME

WHAT TO INCLUDE IN AN INDUCTION PROGRAMME

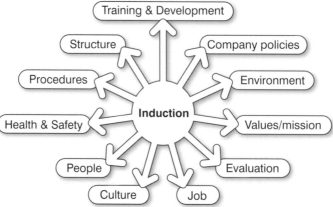

When you have clear objectives for your induction, you must then decide what information you need to support these aims.

WHAT TO INCLUDE IN AN INDUCTION PROGRAMME

DEVELOPMENT ACTIVITY

Undertake a staff survey to find out:

- What people found useful during their first few months on the job
- What people did not find useful
- What could have been done to make their integration easier
- What they found useful at other companies they have worked for

Don't forget to include:

- People who have been promoted to a new job
- People who have transferred to a new department or location
- People in regional or international offices

Think about yourself – what would have been useful in your first few weeks?

WHAT TO INCLUDE IN AN INDUCTION PROGRAMME

THE FOUR Ps

The sort of information that people generally find useful falls into four categories:

- **Place** – structure of company and physical surroundings
- **Policies** – how to behave in various situations
- **Position** – their job role and how it fits into the company
- **People** – who they will be working with

Information about all four Ps will show the
newcomer the best way to fit in.

WHAT TO INCLUDE IN AN INDUCTION PROGRAMME

THE FOUR Ps: *PLACE*

Employer information

What do you know about the history and aims of your employer?

How does your role contribute towards achieving these aims?

Many people are unable to answer these questions. However, this information is essential if newcomers are to be motivated and clear about their roles. Information about the employer should cover:

- A brief history
- Aims and objectives
- Organisational structure
- Products or services
- Function and role of the departments

THE FOUR Ps: *PLACE*

Physical surroundings

This aspect is easily overlooked but is very important for someone who is not familiar with the work surroundings and who may find it embarrassing to keep asking where things are. Therefore, a tour is essential, no matter how large or small the site may be. Include:

- Entrances and exits
- Canteen or location of coffee machines, kitchens
- Notice boards
- Post room
- Fax and photocopier
- First aid room
- Cloakrooms
- Other sites, factory, shops

You may add or leave out what is or is not applicable to your premises.

THE FOUR Ps: *PLACE*

Development activity

If you do not have a formal **welcome pack**, you can begin to create one by:

- Sending out short questionnaires to people, asking for information on what they do and whether they have any documentation or leaflets to assist you
- Gathering information such as annual reports, brochures and organisation charts
- Asking your contacts in other companies what they have and, if they are willing, allowing you to look at their information

You'll be surprised just how much information exists that you didn't know about!

Remember:

- Refer back to the survey done previously to find out what it is that people would find useful
- Use this information in your welcome pack
- Consider the medium to use (remember your GAME plan) – should it be a hard paper copy? Should it be part of a company CD-ROM? Should it be available on the intranet?

WHAT TO INCLUDE IN AN INDUCTION PROGRAMME

THE FOUR Ps: *POLICIES*

The information on policies covers procedures and guidelines on what to do in various situations. It can include any of the following:

Personnel policies

- Terms and conditions
- Benefit entitlement
- Grading structure and salary payments: when, calculation, how paid
- Sick leave rules
- Holidays
- Grievance and discipline
- Family-friendly
- Training and development

WHAT TO INCLUDE IN AN INDUCTION PROGRAMME

THE FOUR Ps: *POLICIES*

Communication policies

- How staff are informed
- Staff representative body
- Consultative arrangements
- Notice boards
- E-mail
- Intranet
- Meetings
- Trade union
- Internal TV channel
- Informal social gatherings

Health and safety policies

- Safety rules
- First aiders/equipment
- Location of fire exits
- Policy on smoking
- Accident reports

THE FOUR Ps: *POLICIES*

Development activity

When deciding what to include in an induction programme, it often comes to light that there is a lack of documentation giving guidance to staff and that the only way to learn is through mistakes or word of mouth.

Your induction team could, therefore, gather any forms or guidelines that already exist and develop the rest with the assistance of the people responsible for that particular area.

Ensure all your guidelines follow a consistent format and clearly indicate:

- The objective for having the policy
- The step by step procedure
- The person responsible

Remember to use **GAME** (see Introduction).

THE FOUR Ps: *POSITION*

Job description

Newcomers should be informed exactly what is expected of them so that they have every opportunity to do a good job. The best way to do this is through a job description. This should include:

- An explanation of the team/department role
- The main function of the position
- The key tasks or responsibilities
- The interface with other people/departments
- The equipment/facilities to be used
- What the newcomer will be working on initially

WHAT TO INCLUDE IN AN INDUCTION PROGRAMME

THE FOUR Ps: *POSITION*

Training and development

If your company trains and develops staff and monitors their development, you will need to go through:

- How development needs are assessed
- What development is available
- How to access the information about the available opportunities
- Who is responsible
- What the procedure is for requesting development

Don't forget, development includes: coaching, mentoring, work experience, books, seminars, articles, courses, distance and remote learning.

WHAT TO INCLUDE IN AN INDUCTION PROGRAMME

THE FOUR Ps: *POSITION*

Performance management

Whatever method you have of reviewing staff performance, whether formal or informal, it is important that newcomers are made aware of this so that they know what to expect.

Give them:

- A copy of all the relevant documentation used – this includes forms and guidelines
- An explanation of the procedure
- Details of who is involved
- Timings when the process occurs
- Details of their involvement/preparation
- Details of your development workshop about performance management that they should attend

Remember, performance management doesn't just mean an annual appraisal, it commences with induction and the setting of objectives. It also includes the probation meeting, the annual appraisal and, possibly, an informal six-month appraisal.

WHAT TO INCLUDE IN AN INDUCTION PROGRAMME

THE FOUR Ps: *PEOPLE*

When you first started your job, there were probably a lot of people you wished you had met earlier who would have made it easier for you to settle in. Who specifically can be of help to the newcomer will vary according to that person's role. Generally, it would be beneficial to meet and spend time with:

- The line manager
- Whoever deals with personnel issues such as pay and holidays; in some cases this may be the line manager
- A member of the senior management team
- Team members, if working in a team
- Any other members of staff that the newcomer will be interfacing with
- Clients if relevant
- Someone doing a similar job

HOW TO IMPLEMENT INDUCTION

HOW TO IMPLEMENT INDUCTION

THINGS TO THINK ABOUT

Once you have got a committed team of people prepared to contribute and have received feedback on what information/activities would be useful, the most important part is to decide how to deliver this so that it is beneficial to the recipients. This means thinking about:

- Structure
- Length
- Timing
- Fitting in with company culture
- Method of delivery
- Technology
- Location (depending on whether people are at head office, in a regional office, in an international office)

STRUCTURE

There are two main formats that induction can have:

- Modular
- Continuous

A modular format involves splitting the information into blocks and delivering it at different stages during the first few months of a newcomer joining. Some companies may have an induction that lasts six months; others continue for up to a year.

The alternative is to do the induction continuously over a period. This can range from one day to two weeks in some big organisations.

STRUCTURE

PROS & CONS OF EACH STRUCTURE

Modular		Continuous	
Pros	**Cons**	**Pros**	**Cons**
Information given over time so able to assimilate better	Takes longer	All done in one go so less disruptive	May be too much to take in
You can pick and choose which parts are relevant depending on the newcomer	May have to wait for appropriate part to come round again	Everyone given the same information at the same time	May not always be relevant
Opportunity to try out new knowledge before receiving more information	May limit the amount of work that can be done	Able to do all aspects of the job since given all information at once	May not do tasks well owing to information overload

HOW TO IMPLEMENT INDUCTION

LENGTH

The length of the induction programme depends on:

- Structure of the company
- Structure of the programme
- Amount of information/activities involved
- Newcomer's role
- Newcomer's previous experience
- Whether newcomer has been promoted, transferred or newly appointed

This will differ from company to company.

CULTURE

All companies, like people, have specific features and characteristics that make them what they are. As part of the induction programme, these characteristics need to be conveyed to newcomers so that they can integrate with ease.

They fall into three categories:

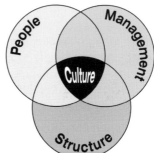

CULTURE

Development activity

With your induction team, go through the list of questions on the following pages to identify your company culture.

CULTURE

People

- What is the typical background; are they all graduates, professionals, etc?
- What is the largest age group?
- What is the ethnic mix?
- What is the male/female ratio?
- What is the dress code?
- What is the average length of service?
- What is the social calendar like?

CULTURE

Structure

- Number of staff?
- All in one location or different sites?
- Is the company 'flat' or are there many layers of management?
- To what extent is technology used?
- Is the layout open plan or individual offices?
- Modern or traditional offices?
- Private or public sector?
- What are the main operations?
- What is the main activity: selling, producing, consulting, etc?

CULTURE

Management

- What are the mission and key objectives of the company?
- Are there rules and regulations?
- Does the company use policies and procedures?
- How is information communicated?
- What is the management style?
- What happens when people make mistakes?
- What issues generate excitement/energy?
- Are there job descriptions and organisational charts?
- Is there a training and development strategy?

MANAGEMENT

CULTURE

Integrating your culture into the induction

By going through the questions on the previous pages, you can devise a cultural profile of your organisation. Below is an example of a cultural profile for a public relations company:

Informal, private sector, non-bureaucratic company, concerned with managing the public profile of a range of pharmaceutical products and where the people who provide the service are responsible for all aspects of the work.

When putting your cultural profile together, it is essential that all those involved agree that this is a true representation of the company.

CULTURE

Integrating your culture into the induction: practical tips

Once you have your cultural profile, use this to design and deliver an induction programme that demonstrates the company culture to the newcomer.

- If there is a formal dress code, make sure all involved represent this
- If there is an in-house written style, make sure that the tone, layout and pitch of the documentation and presentations reflect this
- Be honest – don't present a false picture of the company
- Be well organised and businesslike if that is what you want to portray
- Try to get a cross-section of staff involved to represent the company
- If you are a high-tech company, use technology as much as you can: for example, a company CD-ROM for all the induction and underlying company information; remote learning for company specific training
- If you are a multi-national company, ensure this is reflected in the programme, for example, is English a first or second language; is the same induction programme appropriate for the UK, European and US workforces?

HOW TO IMPLEMENT INDUCTION

METHOD

To ensure your induction is interesting for the newcomer, use a variety of methods to convey the message. By doing this, the newcomer will:

- Learn faster
- Build on their knowledge
- Retain the information

Therefore, include in your induction programme:

- Quizzes
- Treasure hunts (virtual or real!)
- Team competitions

Some companies even have an induction crossword to complete!

Remember, newcomers will learn quicker if the induction process has an element of FUN!

HOW TO IMPLEMENT INDUCTION

METHOD

Written material

This is usually the best method of imparting initial information about the company role and its terms and conditions. Ideally, written information should be issued before the newcomers actually start so that they have time to digest it. If necessary, they can ask for clarification once they start work. Remember:

- Think of the technology to use – is the written material to be sent as a hard paper copy or is it more effective to send a CD-ROM?
- Update regularly
- All information must be expressed in company style
- It must reflect your company culture
- It should be easy to follow and understand
- Use tables, diagrams and charts if these make the information clearer
- All information must be relevant to the newcomer
- Use photos of key people if you can
- Direct the newcomer to your website
- Make it exciting – if you find it boring, so will the newcomer!

METHOD

Coaching

Coaching is a day-to-day activity carried out by the line manager. For coaching to be a success there are some points to bear in mind:

- The manager must be committed and see this as part of his or her job
- The manager must have the right combination of knowledge, skill and attributes
- The coaching must be a structured two-way process
- The location of the newcomer must be taken into consideration
- The use and type of technology to aid this coaching needs to be discussed and agreed between the line manager and the newcomer

HOW TO IMPLEMENT INDUCTION

METHOD

Formal training and development

Use this when the newcomer needs to develop skills that are essential for the job. These could include company-specific IT, company writing style and customer care. When deciding what development is relevant, make sure:

- You have identified all skills and knowledge that need to be covered

- You have tailored the development to suit the newcomer's background, culture, experience and location

- You have considered how the development will be delivered and the most suitable timing

- You have considered what technology will be required and checked that it is available

- You have planned how to test the knowledge gained by the newcomer by use of tests, quizzes and so on

- You have decided how the long-term benefits of the development will be assessed

HOW TO IMPLEMENT INDUCTION

METHOD

Group work

This can be useful for integrating newcomers into the teams they are going to work with. Remember, the team may work in the same location or they may be working virtually, in which case some careful thought and planning will be needed. Group work can include activities such as:

- Team briefings on current projects
- Business games
- Case studies
- Role play
- Away days

For all of these activities, ensure that you have a clear objective – ie: why the team is doing the chosen activity – and some kind of follow-up or action plan.

HOW TO IMPLEMENT INDUCTION

METHOD

The newcomer

It helps to include newcomers in implementing induction. After all, they are there to learn and will do so more quickly and remember more information if you can actively engage them in activities and research. Therefore, as well as using quizzes, questionnaires, crosswords, treasure hunts and team competitions, during the induction programme, you should consider using drama.

For example, to illustrate the importance of team work, engage them in putting together a play with other newcomers. Or make the venue into a mock cinema and let the newcomers watch a carefully chosen film – remember the popcorn! The next day revisit the film to draw out management lessons.

Alternatively, you could bring in actors to illustrate key areas or be part of role-play sessions. The important point is that fun and participation will aid learning.

METHOD

Visiting different parts of the company

A programme of visits to different departments is useful if it is relevant to the newcomer's job. You must make sure, however, that those being visited are prepared and have a structured programme for the newcomer to follow.

- Explain the objective(s) of the visit
- Explain what the department/office does and how it links with the newcomer's work
- Get the newcomer to shadow a departmental member for a day or two
- Arrange for the newcomer to attend useful meetings or events that demonstrate the work of the department
- Ask the newcomer to write a short follow-up report on the visit

Remember, that this may depend on the location of the newcomer and another option, with today's technology, may be a virtual visit to another office via a company CD-ROM or a video-link, for example.

HOW TO IMPLEMENT INDUCTION

METHOD

Work placement

Some companies organise work placement for 1-2 weeks
in different parts of the organisation, to enable
the newcomer to understand what each part
does and how they all fit together. This is
useful in cases where you have:

- A factory
- Regional offices
- Shops
- Press office

The placement should involve some shadowing and
some actual work. It is particularly useful for new
managers who are going to be responsible for the
people working in those parts of the company.

HOW TO IMPLEMENT INDUCTION

METHOD

Buddying

Buddying is a really useful way of imparting *unofficial* information to a newcomer. It is very effective if done carefully and doesn't require a lot of resources in terms of organisation and cost.

A buddy is usually someone doing a similar job or of similar status who volunteers to take care of a newcomer for his or her first few months.

The buddy must:

- Be knowledgeable about the company
- Be willing to put time aside to spend with the newcomer
- Have a sympathetic ear when the newcomer is having difficulties

METHOD

Presentations

Presentations are commonly used for induction training as they can be more interesting than written material and can cover a considerable amount of detail. For better retention, break up your presentations into half-day blocks.

Remember:

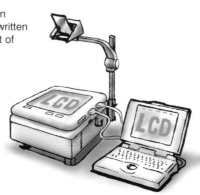

- All presenters should be trained
- All visual aids should be uniform in appearance and in the company house style
- Check all material is up to date before using it

METHOD

Presentations: example

Time	Topic	Method	Speaker
9.30-9.45	Coffee and registration, issue handouts	Handouts	Facilitator
9.45-10.00	Introductions and ice breakers	Activity	
10.00-10.30	History of the company Mission, aims and objectives	Talk using slides/company video Question and answer	Managing Director

Presentations: example (Cont'd)

Time	Topic	Method	Speaker
10.30-11.15	Outline of services/products, how company works to serve its customers, outline of different departmental roles	Talk Question and answer	Manager of department
11.15-11.30	Coffee break		
11.30-12.00	Health and safety – fires, first aid, security	Video	Health and safety officer (or whoever deals with this)
12.00-12.30	Training and development: what is available, how this is reviewed, who is responsible	Talk using slides	Training person
12.30-1.00	Activity (eg: quiz) Questions Evaluation	Activity	Facilitator
Lunch	Invite staff to meet newcomers		

METHOD

Presentations: tips to add interest

- Give information to attendees in advance so that they have a chance to read through material beforehand

- Allow for questions at the end of each presentation - ask attendees to prepare some in advance or they may sit there and look blank

- Encourage participation by using ice breakers and other activities

- Do an activity at the end, such as a quiz, to test knowledge

- Ensure topics and speakers involve all attendees

HOW TO IMPLEMENT INDUCTION

METHOD

Presentations: tips to avoid common errors

- Inspect all speaker slides, handouts, etc beforehand to ensure that:
  - they are laid out in a consistent manner
  - they are up to date
- A few days before the event, remind speakers and newcomers of date, time and place
- Have an activity or topic to fall back on in case a speaker is late
- Check all equipment and room layout the day before; don't leave it to the last minute
- Ensure the room is laid out in a way that encourages discussion - for example, horseshoe shape or round a table, not rows of seats
- Ensure all involved know how to use the equipment

METHOD

Pilot

Never take a newcomer through your induction process without first running a pilot scheme. This will allow you to check without embarrassment that:

- You have the right amount of information
- The delivery method is suitable
- There are no gaps
- The handouts, slides and other material are understandable
- Those involved know exactly what they are doing
- It works!

NOTES

WHEN & WHERE INDUCTION SHOULD TAKE PLACE

WHEN & WHERE INDUCTION SHOULD TAKE PLACE

WHEN

Returning to Maslow's theories, you will remember that people have a hierarchy of needs and that they cannot move on to the next stage unless the previous need is satisfied. These needs can be used as a guide to what information should be given at what stage.

Before starting	where to go and what to do
First day	company and job information
Next few weeks	activities to establish relationships
Longer-term needs	feedback on objectives, training and development

BEFORE STARTING

Induction starts the moment a person knows they have got the job. As soon as they have accepted, you want them to know how glad you are that they have accepted and how much you are looking forward to them working with you. So send a welcome letter as soon as possible as they may not start for a few weeks.

In the letter state:

- How pleased you are that they are joining you

- What time to arrive on the first day
  (usually later than normal hours)

- Where to go – reception location

- Who to ask for – whoever will be meeting and greeting them first

- What will take place on their first day
  (timetable of activities)

BEFORE STARTING

Also indicate what you would like the newcomers to bring with them. This may include:

- P45
- Bank details

Some information about the company should also be sent, including:

- Details of benefits
- Organisational charts
- Job description
- Company brochure

This could be part of the welcome pack that you put together earlier.

FIRST DAY

This is your chance to impress the newcomers and make them feel they have made the right decision. They should go home that evening with a smile on their faces, looking forward to the next day. You can do this by ensuring that you have planned exactly how they are going to spend their first day and making sure all those responsible have booked the time in their diaries.

Remember, the first impression is a lasting impression.

The standards you expect of your newcomers will be demonstrated by your actions, so always:

B e on time

L eave enough time

A void interruptions

B ook a room or take them out

FIRST DAY - EXAMPLE

Start late, finish early and focus on basic needs.

Day 1

Time	Person/Activity
10.00	**Iqbal Khan** (line manager) - Welcome, establish rapport, go through job role
10.30	**Iqbal Khan** - Introduce to the team and buddy (10 minutes with each)
11.00	Tour of the building
11.30	**Mary Little** (HR administrator) - Check paperwork, go through company policy
12.00	Lunch with team
1.30	**Team secretary** - Sort out personal work area, stationery, books, IT password, etc
2.00	Give task to begin work on
4.00	**Iqbal Khan** - Feedback on the first day
4.30	Send home

WHEN & WHERE INDUCTION SHOULD TAKE PLACE

NEXT FEW WEEKS

The aim during the first few weeks is to ease the newcomers into their new roles and to enable them to become familiar with their manager and colleagues. Supply information and set tasks with this in mind. Newcomers may be expected to:

- Undergo specific training and development
- Spend time with colleagues they will be interacting with
- Find out more about the company by reading literature, looking at a company CD-ROM, using the intranet (see also page 72-73)
- Set some work objectives with their line manager
- Develop the relationship with their manager through regular feedback meetings
- Visit different sites (if relevant)
- Go through health and safety issues
- Go through company policy
- Undertake work placements
- Shadow others doing the same or similar job

As before, technology may be necessary if multiple locations are involved.

LONGER-TERM NEEDS

Once newcomers begin to settle in, they will be looking for information and activities that will enable them to perform their work at full speed as well as develop themselves. Once the formal induction process is over, there shouldn't be a sudden withdrawal of support. Continue to give support by:

- Ensuring your behaviour and that of your team match the rules given to the newcomers
- Giving regular feedback
- Providing the newcomers with buddies, with whom they can meet to discuss progress, as an alternative to meeting their managers
- Encouraging contribution of ideas from newcomers who can often bring a fresh perspective
- Dealing with any problems at an early stage
- Reviewing performance after 1-3 months
- Setting clear objectives in line with individual and company goals

WHERE

The place where you have your induction is entirely up to you and may also depend on where the newcomer is located. However, bear in mind that for:

One-to-one meetings
It is better to have a private room with no interruptions. This may also include video-conferencing and web-cam meetings, for example.

Group activities
It is usually better to hold these in an external venue where everyone can concentrate without fear of interruptions. Consider hiring a room or going out for lunch.

WHEN & WHERE INDUCTION SHOULD TAKE PLACE

WHERE

Training and development

If you have training rooms, then use these, otherwise book a room outside. You may have the facility to use CD-ROMs, DVDs or remote learning packages for desktop training or, indeed, have a learning resource centre dedicated to training and development.

Work placement

The induction should be 'on the shop floor', where the activity actually takes place.

Always make a special effort to ensure the induction activities are held in the appropriate place. Have a mixture of locations: the office as well as off-site.

EVALUATING
YOUR INDUCTION

EVALUATING YOUR INDUCTION

WHY

If you are going to take the time and make the effort to put together an induction programme, you must similarly take time and effort to evaluate it, to ensure you have met the original objectives, and to identify any areas for improvement. The evaluation process starts with the pilot, at which point you should check the content, clarity of the information and the delivery.

The evaluation of the actual induction should check that the newcomers:

● Have understood the company structure, products/services, clients and culture
● Know what action to take in various situations (eg: fire, taking holidays, being appraised)
● Have understood their roles and how these fit with company aims
● Have received relevant training and development and are utilising this
● Have met the appropriate people (either face-to-face or virtually) to assist them in their roles and in different situations

Go back to your objectives for having an induction and use these as a basis for your evaluation.

EVALUATING YOUR INDUCTION

HOW

Testing the newcomer

Throughout this book the *fun* side of the induction programme has been emphasised.

All of these fun methods (quizzes, treasure hunts, team competition, crosswords) can be used as part of your evaluation throughout the newcomer's induction. They can show you:

- How well the newcomer understands the company
- How they may deal in certain situations
- Whether they will find it easy to find out information from other parts of the company
- Whether they understand what to do when under threat of a fire or a bomb
- How well they are taking on board the newly acquired skills, such as IT... *and even*
- How well they work in a team and how good their research skills are!

EVALUATING YOUR INDUCTION

HOW

There are several methods that can be used for evaluation and it is best to try more than one to get an accurate picture.

Questionnaires

These can be given to the newcomers once their induction is over. Suggested questions:

1. What were your expectations of the induction programme?
2. Were these met?
3. Did you feel you had your induction in time?
4. What did you find most useful?
5. What did you find least useful?
6. How would you rate the people involved in delivering your induction?
   (List all involved and get newcomers to grade them.)
7. What did you think of the location of your induction?
8. What did you think of the methods used? (List these and use a rating system.)

Emphasise that the questionnaires can be anonymous, so no one need be uncomfortable about expressing an honest opinion.

EVALUATING YOUR INDUCTION

HOW

Checklists for attendees

Use these to check how much the newcomer has understood and if there are any areas that need clarification. Indicate that the checklists are not designed to test the attendees but to gain feedback on whether or not there is anything more that can be done for their benefit. Checklists can include:

Meetings activities
What were these and what did you find out from each?

Health and safety
Where is the nearest exit to you?
Where is the assembly point?
What do you do if you discover a fire?

Company information
What is the main service that this company offers?
Who are the main customers?
What are the future aims of the company?
What is the function of your department?

EVALUATING YOUR INDUCTION

HOW

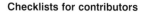

Checklists for contributors

All those involved in delivering the induction programme should have a checklist of what they are to cover. This serves two purposes:

- It ensures all newcomers are receiving consistent information, and

- It can detect if someone has missed an activity or piece of information

Some examples of checklists to use at different stages can be found in the next section.

HOW

Line manager reports

Part of the induction should involve the line manager setting some work objectives with the newcomer. These objectives must be **SMARTER.**

At the end of an agreed period the objectives should be reviewed by the manager and an assessment made of how the newcomer is integrating into his or her new job. This will highlight the benefits of the induction and any areas requiring further assistance.

S pecific

M easured

A chievable

R ealistic

T ime bound

E valuated

R eviewed

EVALUATING YOUR INDUCTION

HOW

Line manager reports: example

Objective	How	By when	Comments on performance
To understand your role and the role of the department.	Read literature. Meetings with manager, meetings with department. Attend induction presentation.	End of April	Has demonstrated an understanding of her role by taking initiative on certain projects. Needs to be involved more in the team to understand other members' work.
To develop new database that is easier to use and consolidates old databases used by department.	Database training course. Meet database users. Offer choice of solutions. Pilot.	End of May	Has produced a new database now being used by team. To be reviewed in a month's time.
To update IT skills in line with company standard.	Go on relevant IT courses.	End of May	Has been on three courses and now using skills to produce work using company templates and style.

EVALUATING YOUR INDUCTION

HOW

Exit interviews

These are usually carried out to identify why a member of staff is leaving. Inadequate induction can sometimes be the cause.

Tips for carrying out exit interviews:

- Carried out by someone who is neutral; not the line manager

- Information treated confidentially

- Questionnaire designed to be used for all staff

- Findings summarised and reported to management on a regular basis

EVALUATING YOUR INDUCTION

HOW

Exit interviews: example

1. What did you enjoy most about your job?
2. What did you not like about your job?
3. How would you rate your workload?
4. Did you receive a good induction into your job?
5. Did you receive the right training and development in order to carry out your job to the best of your abilities?
6. How would you rate your manager?
7. Why are you leaving?
8. What would you improve in the company if you could?

WHAT TO DO WITH THE RESULTS

For evaluation to be of use, you must do something with the findings. Firstly, put the results into a report, summary or table so that it is easy to see the overall effect. This can then be used to:

●   Provide feedback to senior management on a regular basis so that they are able to continue to support induction

●   Improve content and delivery of the induction programme

●   Identify any gaps

●   Give feedback to those who have contributed to the induction programme

NB You can reassure those who have returned questionnaires that results are summarised, so the individual contents are never actually seen by the people they refer to.

COMMON FEEDBACK

Here is some common feedback that you should be aware of when designing your induction:

- Too much information in one go
- Not given at the appropriate time
- Not all information is relevant to all newcomers
- Poor presenters
- Information out of date
- Website being updated
- Parts of the induction should have been arranged earlier

1NDUCTION CHECKLISTS

INDUCTION CHECKLISTS

The following are checklists for all the sections covered. You should go through these when designing and implementing your induction programme.

Why have an induction

Tick those that apply to your organisation: (✔)

To inform about company product/service ☐
To assimilate into the culture ☐
To motivate newcomers ☐
To increase productivity ☐
To reduce staff turnover ☐
To inform about policy and procedures ☐
To involve and empower existing staff ☐
To provide health and safety awareness ☐
To meet colleagues ☐
To understand market/customers ☐

INDUCTION CHECKLISTS

Who to involve (in delivery)

Think about whom you would like to be involved and what they can contribute:

Title	Specialist skills/knowledge
Line manager	
Personnel function	
IT department	
Representative from newcomer's team	
Newcomer's mentor	
A representative from senior management	
Anyone else	

INDUCTION CHECKLISTS

Who to involve (in receiving)

Don't leave out anyone. List all those people who joined, were transferred or promoted since last induction:

Name	Job title	Contract
		Return after maternity leave
		Work experience student
		College leaver
		Promotion

INDUCTION CHECKLISTS

WHAT TO INCLUDE

Preparation before first day

Tick items as you go through: (✔)

Welcome letter	☐
Joining instructions	☐
Job description	☐
Organisational chart	☐
Company brochure	☐
List of what newcomer should bring	☐
Organise IT - password	☐
Desk, stationery, etc	☐
Details of newcomer's induction programme	☐
Inform all those involved	☐
Welcome pack	☐

INDUCTION CHECKLISTS

WHAT TO INCLUDE

On the first day

This can be used to check that newcomers have received all of the information that they should have received:

Item	Person responsible	Date
Personnel		
Meeting at reception		
Checking details – bank, addresses		
P45 received		
Terms and conditions		
Explanation of induction procedure		
Security pass		

INDUCTION CHECKLISTS

WHAT TO INCLUDE

On the first day

Item	Person responsible	Date
IT		
Password		
IT system		
Basics of system		
Line manager		
Introductions		
Go through job description		
Review department function and current projects		
Introduce to buddy		
Lunch		

WHAT TO INCLUDE

On the first day

Item	Person responsible	Date
Colleague		
Tour of office including:		
Toilets		
Exits and entrances		
First aid room		
Notice boards		
Car park		

WHAT TO INCLUDE

Next few weeks

Item	Person responsible	Date
Set work objectives		
Go through training and development		
How performance is measured		
Health and safety procedures		
Company structure		
In-depth IT training		
Telephone system		
Trade unions/staff bodies		
Work placements		
Visits to various departments/sites		

INDUCTION CHECKLISTS

WHAT TO INCLUDE

Meetings and activities

Activity/meeting	Why	Contact name	Date

CASE STUDY

BACKGROUND

LBC are book publishers with a head office in London and six branches round England. A few years ago they underwent a lot of changes which involved a reduction in staff numbers and a flattening of the management structure. They currently have one hundred staff and recruit mainly graduates.

Following these changes, it became evident that staff turnover was increasing and so management decided to do something to improve retention. From exit interviews it was found that a percentage of people were leaving after a year's service because the job had not turned out to be what they expected. It was decided that a new recruitment policy be introduced and, as part of this, new recruits were to have an induction programme.

OBJECTIVES

A team of six staff from different areas of the company was put together to help design and implement the induction. The first thing was to agree the objectives of the induction programme. This was done by using questionnaires and random interviews to find out what people wanted. From this, it was decided that the objectives should be:

- To give an understanding of the company, its function, aims, structure, products, markets and policies
- To give an understanding of the newcomer's job role and how it fits into the company as a whole
- To provide adequate training to enable the newcomer to do his or her job
- To boost morale of current staff and motivate newcomers

PROCEDURE

It was felt that a modular programme would be best in order to accommodate the different needs of graduates, non-graduates and those people who have been promoted and transferred.

The programme required that arrangements be made in preparation for arrival of the newcomer. Items such as desk, phone, computer terminal, password and security pass were all organised beforehand.

Once all had been arranged, a welcome pack was to be sent to the newcomer. This would include company information, joining instructions and induction programme details.

CASE STUDY

PROCEDURE

Module 1   Meeting with personnel to go through terms and conditions.

Module 2   Meeting with line manager to go through team function and job role. Introduction to team members.

Module 3   Half-day presentation given by different department heads and managing director.

Module 4   Individual training.

Module 5   Work placements in other parts of the company.

The induction process starts from day one and continues for six months until the end of the probation period.

CASE STUDY

EVALUATION

The induction programme has been running for one year and the evaluation from the questionnaires and exit interviews has been very positive. The induction team regularly monitors the programme to check that it remains relevant. Two recent changes are:

1. More use of technology – the welcome pack is now available as a company CD-ROM, with relevant company information and also virtual visits to the London and branch offices. It is popular with newcomers, and is quicker and cheaper to update

2. New methods of delivery – desktop training and development is used for improving newcomers' IT skills. The IT department helped develop the remote learning; this includes an on-line quiz immediately after the training and one three months later. After each quiz the IT department makes contact to offer any necessary support.

Line managers feel more comfortable now that new staff have a structured programme to attend during their first weeks.

SUMMARY

SUMMARY

Induction Team

- Gather some volunteers to assist in development and design

- Agree your **GAME** plan:

    Goal

    Audience

    Media

    Expression

Objectives

- Decide what the main objectives are. Include:

    Company
    Team
    Individual

- Remember, the main aim is to **WIN**:

    Welcome

    Integrate

    Navigate

SUMMARY

Who ⟹

Decide who is to:

- Deliver
- Receive
- Train those delivering

What ⟹

Design a questionnaire to find out what people would have found useful.

Divide your findings into the four **P**s:

Place
Policy
Position
People

SUMMARY

How ➡

- Decide on modular or continuous format
- Put together your company culture profile
- Use a choice of methods for delivery to suit different needs
- Run a pilot

When/where ➡

- Using Maslow's theory as a guide, decide on what should be given when
- Remember **BLAB:**

  B e on time
  L eave enough time
  A void interruptions
  B ook room or restaurant

SUMMARY

Evaluation

Use several methods including:
- Questionnaires
- Manager reports
- Quizzes
- Treaure hunts
- Team competitions
- Crosswords
- Checklists
- Exit interviews

Ensure that you use your results to maintain and improve on your induction success.

RECOMMENDED READING

'A Good Start: Effective Employee Induction'
by Alan Fowler, published by CIPD

'How to design and deliver induction training programmes'
by Michael Meighan, Kogan Page

'New Employee Orientation',
by Charles Cadwell, Kogan Page

"When you are inspired by some great purpose, some extraordinary project, all your thoughts break their bonds. Your mind transcends limitations, your consciousness expands in every direction and you find yourself in a new great and wonderful world"

Patanjali

About the Authors

Ruth Sangale BSc MCIPD

Ruth runs her own HR outsourcing service, The HR Dept Ltd. She has over 15 years' HR experience in a range of industries in both large and SME organisations. Ruth has worked at senior level as an HR generalist gaining a wealth of knowledge and experience in recruitment, employee relations, change management, HR policy and training. Ruth is passionate about enabling people to get the most out of their work. She believes that providing employers with support, information and guidance to get the best out of their staff, can contribute to a company's continued success.

Philippa Webster, Chartered FCIPD

Philippa is the founder of Interpersonnel (HR) Ltd and is a Director of the company and works as an HR consultant. She specialises in induction, performance management and review, management development and aspects of employment law including terms and conditions, policies and procedures. Philippa works, in the main, at senior level but also provides support to other levels through one-to-one coaching and workshops. She firmly believes that all organisations need HR support and that it should be integral to the core running of any business. Philippa is a prolific writer and has had many articles published. She also contributes to various HR publications.

Contacts

Ruth Sangale
The HR Dept Ltd, Unit 1, Parklands,
Railton Rd, Guildford, Surrey GU2 9JX
Tel: 0845 634 9150 Mob: 07762740188
Web: www.hrdept.co.uk

Philippa Webster
Interpersonnel (HR) Ltd, HR Consultants,
212 Piccadilly, London, W1J 9HG
Tel: 020 7917 6799 E-mail: info@interpersonnelonline.com
Web: www.interpersonnelonline.com

ORDER FORM

Your details

Name _____

Position _____

Company _____

Address _____

_____

_____

Telephone _____

Fax _____

E-mail _____

VAT No. (EC companies) _____

Your Order Ref _____

Please send me:

		No. copies
The Induction	Pocketbook	
The _____	Pocketbook	
The _____	Pocketbook	
The _____	Pocketbook	
The _____	Pocketbook	

Order by Post

MANAGEMENT POCKETBOOKS LTD

LAUREL HOUSE, STATION APPROACH,
ALRESFORD, HAMPSHIRE SO24 9JH UK

Order by Phone, Fax or Internet

Telephone: +44 (0)1962 735573
Facsimile: +44 (0)1962 733637
E-mail: sales@pocketbook.co.uk
Web: www.pocketbook.co.uk

MANAGEMENT POCKETBOOKS